HOME BREWING

A DIY Guide For Creating Your Own Craft Beer
From Scratch

RICHARD ALTMAN

Table of Contents

INTRODUCTION

Congratulations on purchasing *Home Brewing: A DIY Guide To Creating Your Own Craft Beer From Scratch* and thank you for doing so.

The following chapters will discuss home brewing and all of the work that goes into it. In the first chapter, we give you a short but detailed history of craft beer and brewing. From the first American craft brewery to the thriving industry today, you will get a tour of the history to better understand the integrity and pride that comes alongside craft beer and brewing. Home brewers often follow in this tradition.

After that, you'll get a complete overview of the brewing process, with a full guide on equipment, ingredients, and a step-by-step beer brewing guide. We'll also tell you all about different styles of beer and how they differ in the brewing process. As any home brewer can tell you, half the fun of home brewing is being able to use your innovation and creativity to create a new style, or put a spin on an old one. From India pale ales to pilsners, you'll understand the difference in taste and formulation.

Home brewing is a complex and detailed process that requires attention and choices every step of the way. With this book, we hope to enlighten you on some of the basic practices of home brewing as well as some insight into the world of advanced home brewing.

There are plenty of books on this subject on the market; thanks again for choosing this one! Every effort was made to ensure it is full of as much useful information as possible. Please enjoy!

CHAPTER 1

A Brief History of Craft Beer

Craft brewing has been a steadily growing industry for over thirty years, and is generally defined to mean small, independently owned breweries who focus more on traditional brewing methods, flavor, and small batches. Larger, corporate owned breweries focus more on advertising and consistency of taste across huge batches of beer, and often use mechanized brewing methods. For the most part, breweries that fall into the category of "craft beer" breweries were established after the 1970s, as the beer industry was heavily regulated before this.

The Start of the Craft Brewing Industry

The revival of craft brewing in the United States is attributed to a few things. First, the Anchor Brewing Company was a brewery that initially opened during the California Gold Rush in 1896. It was owned by Ernst F. Baruth, and originally produced what has become known as steam beer or California common beer. This particular type of beer uses lager yeast without proper refrigeration, producing a beer that is much more carbonated than other types of beer.

Despite various fires at the brewery and Prohibition from 1920 to 1933, Anchor Brewing Company remained in business to sell its steam beer p0st-1933. However, though it survived through several hardships, the brewery began to suffer lower sales as the country's beer preferences changed. In the 1950s, it nearly closed several times because of this (and actually did close once in 1959). In 1965, it suffered its closest call yet, simply because the owners of the brewery lacked equipment and expertise. They also did not maintain an adequate level of cleanliness during the brewing process, causing the beer to become sour.

That same year, however, the brewery was bought out by Frederick Maytag. Though Maytag would have to learn brewing entirely from scratch and replace much of the equipment, he did manage to turn the brewery around to properly produce *Anchor Steam* in 1971. Though the beer initially was only sold as a draft at local taverns, it was eventually noticed nationally and demand for it increased. Eventually, it became one of the first breweries to regularly produce porter, barley wine, and India pale ale.

After the success of Anchor Brewing Company, New Albion Brewing Company was founded in 1976. New Albion is known as the first craft beer company in America, and was initially opened and owned by Jack McAuliffe. McAuliffe was a home brewer that eventually built his three-story brewery using equipment that he rebuilt and repurposed from various sources. The brewery produced 7.5 barrels of beer per week, and sold a pale ale, porter, and stout. Though the beer gained a positive reputation and was reviewed well by many national publications, New Albion did not produce enough in order to make a profit, and closed in 1982.

However, despite the repeal of Prohibition and the opening of New Albion Brewing Company, craft beer was not really revived until 1979, when Jimmy Carter deregulated the beer industry. It had been illegal to sell malt, hops, and yeast to home brewers since pre-Prohibition, effectively discouraging the growth of the industry by preventing home brewers from entering it. Once the industry was deregulated, it paved the way for microbreweries and craft beer to really blossom, as people could now brew small batches of beer from their homes.

The small-batch mindset boomed through the 1980s and 1990s to create the craft brewing industry seen in the 2000s and today. There was also a large increase in Belgian beer importation, which also affected the quickly increasing growth rate of the American industry. In 1979, there were only 90 breweries in the United States; for 2015, the Brewers Association reports that there were 4,269 total breweries. Of these, 4,225 are considered "craft" breweries, which is further divided into the following categories: microbreweries, regional craft breweries, and brewpubs.

A microbrewery is generally defined as a brewery producing less than 15,000 US barrels of beer per year, while a regional craft brewery produces less than 6 million barrels per year but more than 15,000.

Brewpubs are craft breweries with a bar attached where they can directly sell beer to consumers.

Craft brewing today has become a profession and industry steeped with integrity and innovation. Brewers often focus much more on the ingredients and techniques used to brew their beer, and are often encouraged to come up with new styles or put a unique spin on an old style. It is an industry that values the many different voices present in it, and for that reason, it has revolutionized beer brewing in the United States.

Home Brewing: The By-Product of Craft Brewing

Today, as an extension of the craft brewing industry, there is a booming home brewing industry that ranges from the most basic hobbyists to small-scale brewers that produce high-quality beer from the comfort of their own homes. It is an extremely easy hobby to get into that can also be taken to much more advanced heights, depending on how much you pay attention to every step of the process and what kind of brewer you want to be. Home brewers fall into three major categories: extract brewers, partial mash brewers, and all grain brewers. We will be taking a more in-depth look at these brewer types in the next chapter, but for now, here are a few basic definitions.

Extract Brewer

Extract brewers are brewers that work from malt extract. Instead of buying grains and extracting the malt yourself, you can buy dry or liquid malt to save a step.

Partial Mash Brewer

Partial mash brewers use some combination of premade malt extract with their own mash, which is made from pre-ground or home ground grains.

All Grain Brewer

All grain brewers create their own mash, instead of using a malt extract. All grain brewing requires slightly more specialty equipment.

Home brewing has become a popular hobby for beer lovers everywhere, and it's easy to see why. It is great for anyone who enjoys learning about the science of alcohol, and every step of the way allows for creativity. Though many people are afraid of getting into home brewing for fear of infection, this risk is largely negated with proper cleaning and sanitizing techniques throughout the brewing process. The best part of home brewing, however, is that even if you do not find that you are particularly good at it, you will learn plenty about beer along the way and develop a new appreciation for any craft beer that you try.

CHAPTER 2

Theory of Beer Formulation and Design

While many people drink beer, there are fewer who understand the exact science behind how beer is made, and even fewer who can apply this science to the art form that is home brewing. As we have said in the previous chapter, though the basic scientific process for brewing beer may be the same no matter how you configure it, every step and piece of equipment has a number of options, pros, and cons to consider. When you really get into home brewing, you'll find that the multitude of options allows for creativity every step of the way.

For now, however, we will be going over the basic science of making beer without getting too much into the step-by-step process, which will be covered in a later chapter. For this, we will need a basic idea of how alcohol is made. There are many different kinds of alcohol, some consumable, and some not. The alcohol you use in a medical situation is very different from the alcohol that you consume.

Consumable alcohol is actually what is known as ethanol, or ethyl alcohol. This type of alcohol is produced by yeast through the fermentation of grains and fruit. When consumed, ethanol produces a number of psychoactive and psychomotor effects, and it has some level of addictiveness. In its purest form, ethanol is odorless, tasteless, and flammable, and can be used for a variety of functions. For example, many thermometers are made with alcohol because it has a very low freezing point.

Since the dawn of time, people have discovered that any number of plants can be fermented with yeast to produce alcohol. For example, whisky is typically produced with some kind of grain – barley is the most commonly used grain, but there is also rye whisky, wheat whisky, and bourbon, which are produced with corn. Wine is made from fermented grapes, rum is made from fermented sugarcane, and vodka is often made from fermented potatoes.

About Yeast and Alcohol Production

Yeast is a single-celled fungus that likes to eat sugar. Fermentation is essentially when a strain of yeast is introduced into an environment in which some amount of fruit or grain has been somehow mixed with water (there are many different ways this occurs), and the yeast then eats the sugars present in the mixture. Once the yeast has consumed the sugar, it produces a few byproducts, including carbon dioxide and ethanol. In baking, yeast is used to make bread rise, because as it releases carbon dioxide into the dough, it cannot escape the dough, causing it to rise. In making alcohol, the yeast is used to produce ethyl alcohol and if necessary, make the drink carbonated.

Once the alcoholic content of a mixture is high enough, however, the yeast cannot survive in the mixture any longer and dies off, leaving us with the beginnings of a delicious drink. This cutoff is around 15% alcohol. The longer a strain of yeast is left to consume the sugars, the stronger the alcoholic drink. For liquor, fermentation must give way to distillation in order to produce a drink with higher alcohol content because the yeast dies. For example, both whisky and beer are made with barley, except whisky is distilled after fermentation to remove the water content and make the drink stronger. It is then aged for some period of time for taste. However, the steps leading up to the distillation of whisky are the same as the steps to make beer.

Barley and Beer

Beer is not just made from soaking barley in water and adding some yeast, however. The barley must be partially sprouted, heated, dried, and cracked so that the enzymes that break down the grain into sugar can be isolated. This process is known as malting. The grain is first soaked in water so that it begins to sprout, then is quickly dried so that the sprout dies. This develops the enzymes in the barley that will ultimately convert the starch present in the grain into sugar.

When the barley has been malted, it is then steeped in very hot water, similar to making tea. As it steeps, the enzymes in the grains break them down to release the sugars. This mixture is commonly known as the mash. The mash is heated evenly and stirred often so that the malt does not scorch to the bottom of the vessel. Once the heating process is completed (there are many steps involved in this), the liquid is then strained from the mash. This liquid is known as wort. It is sticky and very sweet, as all of the sugars from the grains are dissolved in it.

After brewers have produced wort, they then boil it for an hour while adding hops and other spices to it for flavor. Hops are added to cut the sweetness of the wort and add flavor, and depending on how much hops are added, the end result can be very bitter or very sweet. This is often the difference between styles of beer. Hops are also a preservative, which is how their use came about in beer. India pale ale, for example, was created by sailors who were attempting to preserve their beer for long ship rides between England and India. By adding a lot of hops, they could preserve the beer for longer, though the end result is a bitter beer. The flavor of hops is also dependent on where it is grown.

The usage of hops in beer is pretty recent, and prior to using hops, a variety of different spices and plants were used to offset the sweetness of wort. Regardless of the hops and ingredients used during the boiling of the wort, the product then undergoes cooling, straining, filtering, and fermentation. The process is slightly different for home brewers – obviously, home brewed beer is not as filtered as commercial beer. Either way, the wort is sealed in a container with a strain of yeast, and then left to sit for a period of weeks. Where this sealed container is stored and how long it is stored is also the basis for many different styles of beer, but either way, the yeast is left to consume the sugar in the wort and expel ethyl alcohol and carbon dioxide.

Because you can't very well leave a sealed vessel to build up carbon dioxide (or else it will explode), the pressure must be relieved in some way (in home brewing, through an airlock), which means that after fermentation, the beer is uncarbonated. After bottling, the uncarbonated beer is either artificially carbonated, or left to carbonate naturally with whatever remaining yeast is left in the mix. This can be done through aging, either over a period of weeks or months.

Home Brewing Beer

Obviously, not everyone can follow the steps for making beer from start to finish – that would require growing your own barley, hops, and spices, malting the barley, and creating the mash, so there are now a few categories of home brewers that are largely dependent on which step in the process they begin. In the last chapter, we gave brief definitions of three different categories of home brewer: extract brewers, partial mash brewers, and all grain brewers. After learning more about the specific scientific process behind brewing beer, we can now go a little more into depth about these types of brewers.

An extract brewer, as we have said, begins brewing with a premade malt extract. This extract can be either dry or liquid, and there are many different types to coordinate with different types of beer. The biggest point, however, is that an extract brewer does not create their own mash with malted barley grains. Essentially, their wort is already made for them, and they simply have to boil it and follow the rest of the steps for making beer. Extract brewing is a great way for home brewers to start, and it requires less specialty equipment than partial mash brewing or all grain brewing. If you brew a lot of beer, however, it can become expensive to buy malt extract every time.

If a home brewer wants to transition to all grain brewing, then one option is partial mash brewing. This simply means that the brewer uses a combination of premade malt extract and their own malt extract (wort). These two are then mixed together during the hour-long boil, and hops and spices are added. This type of brewing allows home brewers to get used to the process of creating the mash with the malted barley grains. It often requires a second brew kettle, but it is well worth it for the extra creativity and control over the final flavor of the beer.

All grain brewing, then, is brewing in which all of brewer's the wort is homemade from malted barley grains. The brewer takes part in every step of the process (except, perhaps, growing the barley itself and artificially sprouting it), and thus has much more creative control over the final product. The grain, in its unextracted form, is also much less expensive than premade malts. Aside from a second brew pot, other specialty equipment may be needed. In this book, we will be focusing on home brewing for extract brewers.

It should also be noted that barley is *not* the only grain used to make beer – there are many different styles of beer that use different grains, including rye and wheat. Wheat beers, in fact, are a very popular style of beer. Many beers are a mixture of different grains. Regardless of the grain used, however, the basic process is the same, and because we will not be getting into partial mash brewing or all grain brewing, there is little need to go into further detail of how wheat or rye is processed into malt. How much of each malt you use is dependent on the style of beer you decide to brew, and in our final chapter, we will discuss the classifications of many different styles.

Now that you understand the scientific process of brewing beer, we can now get into the details about how this process can be completed within the comfort of your own home. The next chapter will talk about the equipment needed to get started with home extract brewing. While many people may find it easier to just go buy a basic home brew kit, we have provided some level of detail for those who want to build their own setup.

CHAPTER 3

Choosing Equipment for Home Brewing

When you search Google for home brewing equipment, you will come across a wide variety of options for equipment. There are many different tools used in the making of beer, and a lot of home brewers may find it easier to start with a kit before they begin. A good home brewing kit usually includes all the equipment you need to brew a batch of beer, and often its own book or recipe to start with. Most kits will also offer the ingredients used for one particular style of beer. However, regardless of the style, you'll likely receive malt extract, yeast, and hops. Sometimes, your malt extract will already be hopped and you will not need any extra hops.

As we have read before, each step in the home brew process affects the quality of the beer you will produce. No matter what you buy to home brew, you will have to be sure to follow all the steps properly in order to produce a batch that will not turn sour. Often, the quality of the beer you produce is dependent on your how closely you adhere to each step and how well you pay attention. If you do not spend enough time sanitizing your equipment, you could very well produce a batch of awful beer.

Of course, beer brewing has been done in backyards and tiny kitchens for as long as beer has been around. Your equipment does not necessarily have to be top of the line in order for your beer to turn out great. What truly goes into a good beer is the effort and passion of the brewer, and even the best equipment can produce a terrible beer in the end (as we know by many big name brands that do not produce great craft beer). What is important to know is that even if your first batch turns sour, or your third or your fiftieth, you can always improve your technique. Every home brewer has had a batch go sour!

Not only that, but for almost all of the equipment, there are a number of options that have their own list of pros and cons and full discussions surrounding them about what the best option is. An entire book could be compiled discussing equipment, but if you're not interested in that you may be better off just buying a kit and working from there. Learning about all of the different equipment available can be overwhelming for beginners, so just investing in a decent kit can save you a lot of time.

In this chapter we have gone into some detail about different equipment and options for those who are interested. Within the next chapter, we will discuss about the ingredients you need to produce a batch of beer.

A Heat Source

In the beginning steps, you will be bringing your malt extract to a boil, therefore you need a good source of heat that delivers consistent heating and can bring a gallon of water to a rolling boil. Of course, you do not need to go out and buy a special heat source just for brewing beer, though you can certainly find one. For the most part, you will find that your home stove works just fine for brewing beer. However, you can also purchase propane stoves for brewing in order to cut your brewing time. Propane stoves are also useful when you want to move your brewing into a room other than your kitchen.

Most stoves will have what is called a BTU rating. BTU means British thermal units, which is essentially how much heat is needed to bring one pound of water up a single degree Fahrenheit. The higher the BTU rating on a stove, the more heat that it produces. Many people also care about how efficient their stove is, i.e., how much fuel is required to produce as much heat as possible. Depending on your needs, there are a variety of different propane stoves on the market, ranging in price from $40 to $150 and up.

When buying a burner, you will also want to notice how the heat is distributed on the bottom of your brew pot. For the most part, the heat should be distributed evenly. You should also pay attention to how large a pot your burner can handle, and how much beer you intend to be brewing. If you are a fan of producing larger batches, then you will need to take the burner's surface area and weight restrictions into account. Many burners will be able to secure your brew kettle right to the top of the burner so that you have a steady surface to work from. Some brewing stoves can also be fitted with extensions so that your pot can be elevated from the ground. If you plan on a more permanent home brewing operation, there are also lots of options for installing separate burners in your home.

You'll find that many propane stoves are quite noisy and put out quite a bit of heat, so standing near the stove when it is boiling your water can be intimidating. However, there are also many benefits of buying a separate stove for brewing. As soon as you go over 5-gallon batches of beer, though, you may want to start looking into higher quality propane stoves.

A Boiling Kettle

Your boiling kettle is the most essential piece of equipment in your arsenal. The entire brewing process will take place inside this kettle, from boiling your initial batch of water to boiling your malt extract. Regardless of the kind of brewer that you are (extract, partial mash, or all grain), you will need a good brewing kettle to get started.

Brewing kettles are sold in a variety of sizes, generally from 8 gallons up. However, as most home brewers will probably tell you, as soon as you start getting into brewing more heavily, you'll quickly find that 8 gallons is simply not big enough. A good size for a brew kettle is 10-15 gallons so you can reduce how often you boil over the kettle. You need the amount of space for the boiling water, plus some.

There are a lot of materials used to craft brew kettles, and it may be hard to understand the benefits of each one. You'll find that there are many cheaper options if you go with an aluminum kettle over a stainless steel one, but even though these options are cheaper, they are certainly not better. The biggest problem with an aluminum brew kettle is that it requires a great deal of maintenance in order to prevent the aluminum from passing on a strange taste to your beer. Many aluminum kettles will have special coatings to prevent this, but as with any pots or pans that have coatings, these require special cleaning ingredients and techniques in order to preserve them.

Most home brewers seem to agree that a stainless steel kettle is best, and lasts the longest. Though this can be a hefty up front investment, it is much better in the long run if you intend to be brewing for a long time. A good, stainless steel brew kettle can last you almost indefinitely if you take care of it, which is less than can be said of aluminum kettles. Unfortunately, not everyone can afford to purchase a large, expensive brew kettle outright, and some people may not even need to brew that much.

If this sounds like you, you may be better off looking into a 3-4 gallon canning pot for ultra-small batches. Ultimately, what buying a kettle comes down to is determining your needs and your goals as a home brewer. An all grain brewer will have very different needs than an extract brewer, and depending on how you intend to be brewing (and how long you intend to be brewing that way), you will want to buy the kettle to suit those needs.

A Spoon and/or Mash Paddle

This particular one seems like it would be fairly simple, but it is not always. At various points in your brewing, you will need to stir your brew, which can be very thick. There are many of different options for this, and for the most part, it seems to come down to preference. The biggest quality in your spoon is simply length. You need a spoon that will reach down to the bottom of your brew kettle and give you several inches above the boil to work with. Having a spoon that does not go very far above your mash will quickly become too hot.

Spoons will usually come in either plastic or stainless steel, while mash paddles are usually made of wood. Plastic can often offer flexibility when unsticking things from the bottom of your brew kettle, while stainless steel is firmer and will allow you to stir thick mashes easily. Plastic spoons generally do not last as long as stainless steel ones. Mash paddles are an entirely different subject. There are several thoughts about the types of wood used for mash paddles as well as finishes, and a good mash paddle is often an investment similar to your brew kettle.

In general, if you use a wood mash paddle, you want to make sure that it is made out of a hard wood. Softer woods have larger pores that will soak up flavor more easily and will also not last as long. Some good woods to go with are maple, walnut, cherry, or hickory, but again, there is a bunch of debate about which is best. Ultimately, what matters are the flavors you want to impart to your beer as well as how long you want your mash paddle to last.

One thing that seems to be agreed on for mash paddles is that they should be pieces of unfinished wood. The finish on a wood can interact with the mash, causing a number of problems, not the least of which is a loss of head on the beer. Food safe finishes do not necessarily work well for beer – at high temperatures, these finishes can still leach into the beer.

For beginners, it might be much easier to just buy an inexpensive, long spoon of the material of your choice. If you intend on home brewing for a while, then it might be time to think of getting a mash paddle.

A Fermenting Bucket or Carboy

Most of the time, when you buy a home brew kit, it will come with a large, plastic bucket, which is called a fermenting bucket. However, many home brewers use carboys, which is essentially an extremely large bottle. There is a lot of debate over which method is better, and there are obviously pros and cons to each.

Firstly, using a carboy allows you to see the fermentation process, rather than having to open your fermentation bucket, which can often introduce contaminants into the beer and spoil the fermentation process. You will need to store carboys away from the light, however. Carboys come in glass or plastic, and the major advantage of using glass is that it is easier to clean and does not need to be replaced often. Unlike plastic, there is less chance of the glass scratching and storing bacteria. Scratched plastic is basically impossible to clean and sanitize properly to brew. Glass also cannot handle temperatures in excess of 100 degrees Fahrenheit and will shatter, so your wort will need to be chilled before being poured into a glass fermenter.

Depending on the size of the carboy, you may need to use what is called a blowoff hose (instead of an airlock) to move foam and excess hops out of the fermenter. A 5-gallon carboy that is the primary fermenter will almost certainly need this, unless you are working with very small batch sizes. 6.5-gallon carboys may not need this. Essentially, you will need headspace, but so long as you use a larger carboy or a bucket, this is not a problem. Blowoff tubes can be quite a hassle and are often annoying for clean up, as they end with another bucket of water. The amount of foam depends on the kind of beer that you are brewing.

Plastic buckets have a lot of obvious advantages – for one, they are usually cheaper than glass carboys. They have a wider opening, so you do not need to funnel hot wort into them the same way that you have to with carboys. You also don't need to break out the turkey baster or wine thief to take a sample from a carboy. Buckets are much easier to handle than carboys.

However, because buckets are plastic, you will need to take extra care when cleaning and handling it to not scratch the bucket. If you scratch it, the scratches can harbor tiny amounts of bacteria that can completely spoil a batch of beer.

At the end of the day, your fermenter comes down to preference and need. If you're running a one person operation, you may find that the ease of handling and bottling that comes with using a large plastic food-grade bucket is better than dealing with a glass (or even plastic) carboy. Whatever you use simply needs to be large enough to hold your batch – generally, 6 gallons and up for your bucket and 6.5 for a carboy. Some people even use both a carboy and a bucket. Every home brewer's setup is different.

A Bottling Bucket or Carboy with Racking Cane and Hose

The bottling bucket is essentially the same thing as a fermenting bucket, except with a spigot attached. If you use a carboy, you will need to use a siphon when transferring your beer to bottles, which can become quite tedious and annoying. A plastic bucket with a spigot attached saves a lot of time and hassle, and even allows you to better control the fill level of the beer.

Many people also use another carboy with a racking cane and a length of hose. The problem many have with this is starting the siphon, which is why auto-siphons exist. Of course, a major plus to using a carboy with a racking cane and siphon is that you can have a glass carboy, and do not have to worry about scratched plastic and beer contamination. If you don't use an auto-siphon, there are many different methods available to get the siphon started. Many people also prefer these tools because they are durable and will last you a long time.

Even if you are not using a carboy and are instead using a plastic food-grade bucket, you may not have a spigot attached and will still end up using the racking cane and hose. None of these things matter particularly for beer quality so long as you sanitize all of your equipment and are extremely careful when you begin siphoning your beer. The advantage to a bucket over a carboy (spigoted or not) is that when you are transferring the beer from the fermenter into the bottling bucket, you can easily create a whirlpool at the bottom of your bucket to better mix your priming sugar, but otherwise it comes down to preference and what's available.

A Bung and Airlock

If you are using a bucket for fermenting, you will not need a bung. A bung is used to seal a carboy. For buckets, you will just use a lid. Whatever you use, however, you will need an airlock. If you were to seal your wort in a container with the yeast and simply leave it, your fermenter could explode. That is all an airlock is for – relieving the pressure inside the fermenter without allowing air in to contaminate the beer inside. There are many different types of airlocks.

One kind is called a three-piece airlock, which dissembles into three pieces for easy cleaning. Another is called an S-shaped airlock, which is, obviously, shaped like an S. The type of airlock you use really comes down to preference – many people say that using an S-shaped airlock is better for secondary fermentation, while the three-piece is better for primary fermentation. Depending on how vigorous your fermentation is, you may find that you prefer a three-piece if beer happens to get into the airlock, since it is much easier to clean. Airlocks are filled with water, sanitizer, or a high-proof alcohol.

Bottles, Caps, and Bottle Capper

This is pretty much self-explanatory – in order to home brew beer, you need glass bottles that you can fill at the end of the process and cap. You can buy empty glass bottles from home brew shops or re-use old beer bottles. The most important thing about your beer bottles is that they are properly cleaned and sanitized. If you are re-using beer bottles, this is especially important. Investing in a decent bottle brush for cleaning is a good idea.

For a 5-gallon batch of beer, you will typically need about 48 12-ounce bottles (and 48 caps). Some home brewers like to use different colored caps to differentiate between batches – this is, of course, up to preference. It is better to use bottles that have not previously been used with twist off caps, as it will be harder to properly seal the beer.

Bottle cappers are a pretty basic piece of equipment – some brewers have bench mounted cappers for ease, but a simple $20 capper that is handheld works just as well, and depending on the material it is made out of, can last a very long time.

Cleaner and Sanitizer

There are a lot of different options for cleaners and sanitizers, but essentially what happens is you will clean your equipment with a cleaner (either by soaking it for some period of time, or scrubbing) and then sanitize it. One of the key deciding factors in whether your batch of beer turns out okay is whether or not you maintained a good cleaning schedule.

When using cleaners, you should just follow the instructions provided and make sure every single piece of equipment that you used is properly cleaned. If you do any scrubbing, it should be done with a soft sponge or cloth to avoid scratching equipment (especially plastic buckets!).

If you do not buy a cleaner specifically for brewing, you should make sure to buy something that is unscented and undyed, as both of these things can affect your beer adversely. If your cleaner needs rinsing, you should be sure to rinse well. Cleaning your equipment soon after you finish brewing is also helpful because often you will find that your ingredients cake on and become much harder to remove without hard scrubbing.

One commonly used sanitizer is called Star San, which can be loaded up into a spray bottle for quick sanitation. It foams up during use and finishes sanitizing in just a couple of minutes. You do not have to rinse it off. You can use bleach, but this requires much more attention and rinsing, and ultimately is a much greater hassle than using a no-rinse sanitizer.

Regardless of what you use, sanitation is absolutely necessary for every piece of equipment after cleaning.

Some Miscellaneous Tools

You will almost certainly end up wanting a Pyrex measuring cup to properly measure out your ingredients, and as usual, this should be properly sanitized during the brewing process. When it comes to the measuring cup, the larger, the better, and even if you do not buy a Pyrex brand measuring cup, you should still be sure to use a **heat-resistant glass measuring cup**.

You will also need a **thermometer** that is properly calibrated and can withstand very high temperatures. It will need to be able to read as low as 40 degrees Fahrenheit and as high as 180 degrees Fahrenheit. A **wine thief or turkey baster** is useful for sampling the beer from a carboy or bucket, and a **hydrometer** is also useful for measuring the gravity of the beer.

Depending on your setup, you may need various sizes and lengths of food-grade tubing, but again, if you are buying a kit, it likely has everything you need right there.

There are many different options available for equipment, and depending on how deeply you want to be involved in the home brewing process, you can spend hours choosing one piece over another. Every single piece has a reason for being there, and every option has its own list of pros and cons as well as general information about it. Your equipment does not determine the quality of the beer you will produce – what determines that, ultimately is your ingredients and the care you put into brewing. Proper cleaning and sanitization techniques are absolutely necessary if you want to brew a good batch of beer, and no matter what equipment you use, you will need to be cleaning and sanitizing every step of the way.

CHAPTER 4

The Basic Ingredients That Go into Beer

You've finally gotten all of your equipment and set up your home brewing area. Maybe you have a pair of carboys and an inexpensive aluminum brew pot, or maybe you have a couple of buckets and a kettle that is stainless steel. Maybe you have some combination of all of these things – regardless of how you've decided to set up your home brew area (or kitchen), you are ready to make some beer.

Most craft breweries focus a lot on the ingredients that go into the beer, and for good reason. Using good ingredients and a good yeast strain can have a large impact on the final taste of the beer. Many breweries also experiment with adding different ingredients to the brew at different points in the brewing process to give the beer different flavors. However, at its core, there are exactly four ingredients to brewing beer.

Water

For all the work that brewers put into beer, it is still primarily made up of water. The very first step in the brewing process is boiling water. One common mistake many first time home brewers make is not paying attention to the quality of the water. If you use regular tap water, you can very easily create a beer with a medicinal flavor because the water is too chlorinated. You should try to use water that has been filtered or distilled, or even use bottled water.

Malt

Malt is actually referring to barley malt, though there are many other types of malt out there. As explained in the second chapter, before we can create the sticky sweet liquid called wort, barley must first be processed into malt. Malting barley is the process of partially sprouting then drying the barley at a high temperature. Since we are focusing primary on extract brewing, you will likely be working with premade malt, which can come in liquid or dry form.

There are also many specialty malts that can be used to introduce new flavors to the beer and create different styles. Barley malt is also not the only malt used to brew beer. There is also such a thing as rye beer or wheat beer. Your malt will be mixed with water and then boiled with hops to create what is known as wort. The amount and type of malt used for home brewing is often referred to as a malt bill.

Hops

Hops were initially used in beer to better preserve it. Prior to the discovery of hops, the sweetness of the wort was often cut with other bitter spices and ingredients. Happily, hops can achieve more than one purpose – cutting the sweetness of a beer, and preserving it better. Hops come in many different varieties depending on where they are grown. The hops used in a beer often are a determining factor in what style of beer will be brewed.

Yeast

Yeast is the tiny, single-celled fungus that does all the work of making beer. By consuming the sugars in the wort, yeast produces ethanol and carbon dioxide, creating the delicious, fizzy drink that we know as beer. Similar to hops, there are many different varieties of yeast, and each one has a specific set of instructions for activation. Some yeast strains will thrive in higher temperatures, while others will thrive in colder temperatures. Some strains are top-fermenting yeast (yeast that sits at the top of a brew to work), while some are bottom-fermenting (yeast that sinks to the bottom). There is also dry and liquid yeast. The yeast used in fermenting a beer is another variable that can be changed to produce different styles.

Aside from the four major ingredients of beer, there are a number of other ingredients that can be added for specific flavors. Blue Moon, for example, is a beer that is brewed with orange peel to impart more of a citrus flavor to the beer. Some brewers may even use coffee or nuts in the brewing process to impart those flavors. The number of ingredients that can be used to brew beer is infinite, and when and how these ingredients are added also has a large impact on flavor.

For your first home brew batch, it is recommended that you use a recipe with the fewest amounts of ingredients possible to reduce the risk that your first batch will turn out sour. If you are an experienced home brewer, you can experiment with many different ingredients to introduce new flavors into your beer.

CHAPTER 5

The Basic Steps of Home Brewing

With all brewing endeavors, there is a basic set of steps that must be followed. Regardless of which brewing recipe you are following, you will need to do the same basic steps. Before brewing, you should first decide what kind of beer you would like to brew. This will be critical in determining which malt, hops, and yeast you use, as well as any additional spices or ingredients. Many traditional styles have a wide range of recipes, depending on your preference.

If you are a more experienced home brewer, you will be able to alter recipes to experiment and create your own styles. Oftentimes, brewers do not quite agree on the guidelines for certain styles, so there are many different guidelines available. Generally, a style is determined by specific flavors present in the beer, bitterness, color, alcohol content, and many, many more factors. For example, the difference between ale and a lager is the type of yeast used (top-fermenting versus bottom-fermenting).

We have not provided a specific recipe for brewing, as there are literally thousands available after a quick Google search. However, we have outlined the basic instructions for brewing a batch of beer. At points, which may differ between styles, we will mention what should be done differently or where you can modify the steps.

Step 1: Cleaning and Sanitizing All Materials

It is vitally important that all the equipment you use to brew beer is properly cleaned and sanitized. If you do not do this, your batch of beer can turn sour. Anything that will be touching the beer after boiling it should be cleaned and sanitized, but cleanliness is also important before boiling. The rule of thumb is simply to clean and sanitize everything used. If you've bought a home brew kit, be sure to check which cleaner and sanitizer is included in the kit, and what the steps are to properly use it. If you use a powdered sanitizer included with a kit, you will probably need to rinse all of your equipment thoroughly once it is finished sanitizing, and you will likely have to wait much longer for it to be properly sanitized. If you have not bought a home brew kit, you should invest in a good no-rinse sanitizer like Star San and follow the instructions included.

Before ever sanitizing your equipment, however, you should clean it with an unscented cleaner and thoroughly rinse it. When cleaning equipment, you should use a soft sponge or cloth in order to ensure that nothing is scratched. This is especially important if your brewing setup involves plastic buckets. Small scratches on the inside of these can harbor bacteria that will completely spoil a batch of beer. Your cleaning technique should ensure that none of your equipment is scratched. Once properly cleaned, your equipment can then be sanitized (sanitizers do not work if the equipment is not already clean).

Step 2: Gathering Ingredients

Once you have decided on a style or recipe, you should gather and prepare your ingredients. The most obvious ingredients are water, malt extract, hops, and yeast. Malt extracts can also be hopped already, so you should pay attention when buying yours to determine if you will need to buy hops on top of the malt extract. Depending on the style of beer you have chosen, you may also have to buy specialty malts.

However, if you are brewing your first batch of beer ever, you should try to choose a simple recipe that does not require much unusual preparation or ingredients. One of the biggest mistakes for first time brewers is trying a style that is extremely difficult to produce and not getting good results because of it. For example, if you are aiming to produce a higher alcohol beer, you will need more yeast and time. Some recipes may call for strange ingredients to be added at strange intervals in the process, which can also be difficult for a beginner. Choose a recipe that is safe and will produce something drinkable.

Step 3: Boiling Water

Your first step in brewing beer is boiling water over your heat source with your brew kettle. The water used for your beer will matter. You will want to filter your water, especially if it is tap water, as chlorine or chloramines will produce unpleasant flavors in the final product of the beer. You can use a charcoal filter to filter your water if your water has chlorine or chloramine, or you can buy bottled, filtered water instead.

In general, one pound of liquid malt extract per gallon of water is a good rule of thumb, though some recipes may call for more or less malt. Your recipe will be more specific on how much water should be boiled, but this will be your first step.

Step 4: Adding and Boiling Malt Extract

Your next step in brewing beer will be to add your malt extract to the boiling water. To do this, you should take the boiling water off of your heat source and add the malt. Your recipe will determine how much malt is added, and whether any specialty malts need to be added. As you add your malt, you should be stirring with your long spoon or mash paddle, ensuring that the malt does not just sink to the bottom of your brew kettle. If it does, it can scorch to the bottom of the kettle.

Once your malt has completely dissolved in the water, you will return your brew kettle to the heat source, and bring to a boil. The boil should be rolling.

Step 5: Adding Hops and Other Ingredients

At this point, you can add your hops and whichever other ingredients you have decided to use for your beer. In fact, many recipes may even call for specific ingredients to be added before initially boiling your malt extract in water. Whatever other ingredients you add, however, you should add hops at this stage in the brewing process. When they should be added depends largely on the style of beer you are brewing as well as the type of hops that you have purchased. Most people, in gathering their beer ingredients, will label hops with the time during the boil that they should be added.

Step 6: Chilling the Wort and Pitching the Yeast

Once you have completed the boil (which can range from 30 to 90 minutes, depending on the recipe, style, and many other factors), you must chill your wort to get it down to yeast-pitching temperature. Yeast-pitching is essentially when the yeast is added to the wort in the fermenter and left to begin consuming sugars. There is some disagreement about when the best time to pitch yeast is – some brewers will say between 70-75 degrees Fahrenheit, while others may say lower and others may say higher. The danger of adding yeast while the temperature is too low is that it may become dormant, while the danger of adding it while the temperature is high is that it could die. You should not pitch any yeast above 100 degrees Fahrenheit.

Good practice is to research the strain of yeast that you are using and follow the recipe to pitch the yeast. Your recipe will either have had you perform a full boil or a partial boil. A full boil is when your entire wort is boiled prior to cooling, meaning that you will likely need a wort chiller to properly cool it or some other method. There are many online. Partial boil is when only some of your final product is boiled (say, 2 gallons in a 5 gallon batch) and then added to some amount of water (preferably similarly filtered, distilled, etc.), and then allowed to cool from there. Whatever method of cooling you use, you should always check the temperature of the wort with a thermometer before ever pitching yeast.

Another factor in chilling the wort is the container in which you do it. You can either chill the wort in your boiling kettle, or chill the wort in the fermenter itself. However, if your fermenter is made of glass, you should not add water that is too hot or it could shatter. Partial boil chilling is great for first-timers that do not have a lot of excess equipment, but brewers should be wary of bacteria that could be introduced into the wort while it is chilling.

The yeast, however, should only be pitched once the wort has been transferred from your boiling kettle to your fermenter. Depending on the fermenter that you have, this could be as simple as pouring your kettle of wort into a wide-mouthed bucket, or using a funnel to pour it into a carboy. Some recipes may call for the hops and other ingredients to be strained out of the wort, while some may call for them to stay. It will largely depend on the style of beer you are brewing and your available equipment.

Once your wort has reached the yeast-pitching temperature in whatever container it may be in, pour in the yeas. Some yeast may require activation prior to adding. Most brewers recommend using dry yeast over liquid yeast. Whatever you are using, it should be fresh. At this stage, you should also take note of the original gravity level of your wort using a hydrometer. This measurement is explained more fully in the next chapter.

Step 7: Seal and Shake Your Fermenter

Once your yeast has been added, you should seal your fermenter. If using a carboy, this should be with a bung and airlock; if using a bucket, you will typically just have a lid and airlock. Your airlock should be filled with either water, no-rinse sanitizer, or a high-proof alcohol like vodka. Many brewers prefer using vodka just in case the airlock leaks to prevent the beer from being contaminated. If using water, you should use the same kind of water that you used for brewing.

If you are using a smaller fermenter, you may need to use a blowoff hose, which is simply a modified airlock. Instead of the airlock, a hose is attached to the top of the fermentation vessel that leads into a different container of water or sanitizer and completely submerged. Blowoffs are used if there is not much room in the top of the fermenter (headspace), or if there is a particularly vigorous fermentation process. The purpose of the blowoff is to siphon away excess krausen, which is produced in a layer atop the brew as the wort ferments.

After properly sealing your fermentation vessel, you should shake it vigorously to give the yeast oxygen to begin consuming the sugars in the malt. This only needs to be done for a minute or two – depending on your batch size, it could be quite heavy. Some people also debate whether the wort should be aerated prior to pitching yeast or after pitching yeast. There are also many different methods for aeration to be found online. It is important for the wort to be adequately aerated so that the yeast can start a healthy growth cycle. Too little aeration can spoil the brew.

Again, this is a largely debated topic among brewers. Your recipe may call for something completely different, and that is okay too. It is important to note that too much oxygen after pitching the yeast can spoil the brew, which is why if you shake it, you should only do it for a minute or two. Whatever you decide, once it has been aerated and sealed, you should store your fermenter somewhere where it will not be disturbed any further.

Step 8: Storing Your Fermenter and Monitoring

Depending on the style of beer you are brewing, this step will vary a lot. As we will learn in the next chapter, lagers are typically stored at colder temperatures and allowed to ferment for longer, while ales are typically stored at higher temperatures for shorter periods of time. This will also depend on the yeast you are using – ale yeast, again, requires higher temperatures (65 degrees Fahrenheit to 75 degrees Fahrenheit, roughly), while lager yeast requires lower temperatures (50 degrees Fahrenheit or lower).

Your fermenter should be stored in an area that will maintain the yeast's specified fermenting temperature steadily. Anywhere where the temperature fluctuates greatly can cause the yeast to become dormant (if it is too cold) or to die (if it is too hot). It is best to monitor the temperature of your fermenter every day in order to maintain consistency. The growth of yeast at the peak of fermentation can also raise the temperature of the wort by as many as 5-7 degrees, so you should take account of that when you store the fermenter as well. One common mistake among beginners is storing the fermenter in a room that is too warm, especially when fermentation really gets going. If you cannot control the temperature of the storage area very well, you may want to choose a strain that will thrive in the conditions you have.

Depending on the fermenter you are using, you will also need to shield your wort from light. Of course, plastic buckets will not allow light in, but if you are using a transparent glass container for your fermenter, you will need to store it somewhere dark.

Fermentation generally will begin anywhere between 12 and 72 hours after you have finished brewing and sealed the fermenter. This is also dependent on what kind of yeast you have used. Liquid yeast can take longer to begin fermenting. The biggest sign of fermentation is a bubbling airlock, but if you are using a glass fermenter, you can look for other signs, like a layer of foam on top of the brew called krausen. Again, if you have used a fermenter without much headspace, you may already see krausen as it is siphoned away with a blowoff tube.

You should not rely exclusively on your airlock to tell you when fermentation is complete or starting. You may not see very many bubbles with the airlock, which could mean that there is not a perfect seal over the fermenter. It could also mean that fermentation has not started. The telltale sign is the layer of krausen atop the brew, but you can also use a hydrometer to check if the specific gravity of your wort has fallen. If it has, then fermentation has likely begun.

You should minimize how often you open the fermenter for sampling, however. Each time you open the fermenter, you run the risk of introducing unwanted contaminants into your beer. Sampling should be done with a sanitized tool (again, at all steps of the brewing process, you should be using properly cleaned and sanitized equipment). You will know for sure if fermentation is complete by checking the specific gravity of the beer.

Once your beer has finished fermenting and has reached the specific gravity level called for by a particular style or recipe, you are ready to go to the next step.

Step 9: Second Fermentation

Not all beers will require second fermentation. This step is merely here as a placeholder in case your recipe calls for it. Whenever you have to rack the beer away from one container to another, you run the risk of introducing too much oxygen and unwanted contaminants to the beer, which can ruin your whole brew. Second fermentation is generally when dry-hopping is done, and may begin less than a week after you have begun primary fermentation. Again, this will largely depend on your style and recipe.

For the most part, it is agreed that one of the best vessels for second fermentation is a glass carboy with very little headspace. Since your primary fermentation will already be complete, there is very little danger of the krausen causing the airlock to pop off. Second fermentation is also where a number of ingredients can be added. When siphoning the beer, it is important to use a sanitized siphon so that bacteria is not introduced into the brew this late.

We will not go into very much detail about second fermentation here as encouragement to try the simplest possible recipe for your first brew. It is an excellent way to create delicious and creative craft beers, but you should make sure you are familiar with the entire beer brewing process before attempting to use a two-stage fermentation process. Another factor here is also whether or not you will lager the beer, which simply means cold conditioning it to clear the beer.

The science of lagering and cold conditioning could fill many books, though most would agree that it makes a beer better. It is generally done after the last fermentation process so that the yeast has time to settle. It often results in a clearer beer, and can drastically alter the flavor. Your recipe may even call for lagering – in fact, if you are brewing a lager, it likely will.

Step 10: Priming and Bottling

At this point, once your beer has finished fermenting, it will be flat and uncarbonated, so you will need to carbonate it and bottle it. Carbonation at this stage is typically achieved by the addition of refined sugar to the beer just before bottling and allowing the remaining yeast to consume it and produce the needed CO_2. The sugar should be well-mixed, and a good rule of thumb is one ounce of sugar for every gallon of beer. For a 5-gallon batch, it will be 5 ounces. However, if you have a maltier beer that is already sweet or if you did not allow the fermentation process to complete, you may find that your end product is too carbonated if you have added too much sugar. It is a good rule to follow your recipe and utilize the many priming sugar calculators online before adding the sugar.

One good way to add your sugar is to boil a small amount of water (about 2 cups for 5 ounces) and dissolve the sugar in it. If you have a bottling bucket, dumb the solution of sugar and water into the bottom, then with your racking cane and siphon, transfer the beer from the fermenter to the bottling bucket, and use the siphon to create a whirlpool in the bottling bucket to mix the sugar. This will reduce the splash. You should ensure that you transfer the fewest amounts of solids (called trub) from your fermenter to the bottling bucket. Some recipes may call for filtration; use whatever equipment is available to you and follow your recipe.

Some brewers may not even transfer their beer to a separate bottling bucket, though it is much easier during the bottling process if you use one with an attached spigot. Whatever equipment you use, after you have added your priming sugar, you can begin transferring your beer to bottles and capping them with your bottle capper. You should try to ensure that the fill level is the same from bottle to bottle and that there is a sufficient amount of space (about an inch) at the top of the bottle.

Step 11: Storing Bottles

Before you are able to drink your home brew, you must let it sit for longer so that the remaining yeast can appropriately carbonate the beer. This is generally done for a week or two somewhere that maintains a steady temperature (much like fermentation). Though some will say to just store the bottles at room temperature, there is also such a thing as bottle conditioning, which means storing the beer in cooler temperatures. Where you decide to store them, and at what temperature they are stored, will largely determine on the recipe and style of beer you are brewing.

After you have stored the bottles for a sufficient amount of time, you are ready to pop open one of your home brewed beers. If you have done everything correctly, you should have a properly (but not overly) carbonated beer that is not sour. From there, you can go on to modify your original recipe as you see fit, or even try something new. The world of home brewing is full of different styles and techniques to try. We have tried to outline the most basic steps of brewing beer here, but there are pros and cons to many different techniques, and home brewers do not always agree on what is best.

In the next chapter, we will give you a short tour of some common styles of beer, and the general guidelines for each.

CHAPTER 6

Brewing Different Types and Styles of Beer

In our final chapter, we will be discussing the differences between different styles of beer. The many steps and variables in the beer brewing process invite creativity and innovation, which has led to the development of many, many styles. In fact, we almost certainly will not be able to cover all of the differences here, but we will attempt to give a broad overview of many common styles. Before we can really go into, however, common measurements of beer must first be explained.

Measuring Beer

In the history of beer, many different measurements have been developed in order to provide distinctions between styles of beer. The Brewers Association typically classifies styles based on five different measurements: original gravity, final gravity, alcohol by volume (ABV), bitterness (in international bitterness units or IBU), and color (based on either the Standard Reference Method known as SRM, or the European Brewery Convention method known as EBC). Each of these measurements are explained below.

Original Gravity

Both measurements of the "gravity" of a beer have to do with density. The most common scale used to measure density is the specific gravity scale, which is simply the density of a liquid relative to the density of water. This is measured using a hydrometer. In this scale, the specific gravity of water is 1.000. Ethyl alcohol, in its purest form, has a specific gravity of 0.789. Obviously, the more sugar present in the liquid, the denser the liquid is, creating a specific gravity measurement greater than 1.000. The presence of ethanol, meanwhile, decreases the density of the liquid. Original gravity refers to the specific gravity measurement of the wort before it is fermented with yeast.

Final Gravity

Final gravity, then, is the measurement of the specific gravity of the beer after the wort is fermented. When compared to the original gravity of a beer, brewers can tell how much of the sugar in the wort was converted into alcohol.

Alcohol by Volume

By extension, alcohol by volume is calculated by comparing the original gravity of the wort to the final gravity of beer to see how much sugar was converted into alcohol. There are two equations for calculating alcohol by volume using original and final gravity measurements. They are as follows:

$$ABV = 135.25(OG-FG)$$

This equation is typically used for beers below 6% alcohol.

$$ABV = 133(OG-FG)/FG$$

This equation is more accurate for beers over 6% alcohols.

Bitterness

As we already know, the addition of hops to wort is meant to cut the sticky sweetness of the beer so that it is drinkable and so that it will last longer. Hops are an integral part of the brewing process. It follows that home brewers can change the amount and type of hops added in order to produce different flavors in the beer, and for this, many bitterness scales have been developed to rate how bitter a beer is. By far the most commonly used scale, however, is international bitterness units (IBU).

IBU attempts to quantify bitterness by measuring the amount of iso-alpha acids in beer using a technique called spectrophotometry. Unfortunately for most home brewers, this requires an entire laboratory to determine accurately. That is why home brewers have developed a variety of equations to estimate IBU based on a number of factors, most notably hops utilization during brewing. Hops that are added for the full duration of brewing, for example, produce a more bitter beer, while hops that are added late tend to affect the aroma of the beer over the taste. There are a number of online calculators that can be used to estimate IBU.

If you are truly interested in producing more bitter or sweet styles, it is certainly good to understand the basics of IBU, but it is unlikely that you will be able to really very accurately classify your home brew beer based on this scale. Luckily, brewing styles based on this scale is as easy as looking up a recipe to produce a beer that will have the bitterness profile of the beer you desire.

Color

Color is a major determining factor in style as well, and luckily, it tends to be a fairly obvious distinction between beers. Two common scales have also been developed for color, called the Standard Reference Method (SRM) and the European Convention Method (ECM). Both methods also utilize a spectrophotometer to measure the color of beer or wort. The ECM scale also measures haze in beer, which is known as turbidity. Again, since most home brewers will not have access to the lab equipment required to measure the color of a beer, other approximate methods are used.

Luckily, color is much easier to estimate than bitterness, and most home brewers can simply make use of a color card for reference. If you purchase a color card for your home brews, it is better to buy the card from a home brew store rather than print it out, as color cards will differ from printer to printer. It is also worth noting that even with the proper equipment, measurements of color can still be inaccurate.

For extract brewers, it is more likely as well that beer will turn out to be darker than expected, simply because malt grows darker over time and because of caramelization that can occur during boiling.

These are the major measurements used to classify beers. Each of these measurements can be manipulated during the brewing process, and through their manipulation, different styles of beer are created.

The final two basic distinctions of beer are lager and ale, and some beers are even a hybrid of the two. The rest of this chapter will be divided into lagers and ales, and then some common styles will be explained within these two headings. There are typically more ale styles than lager styles, though this is by no means an exhaustive list. If we've missed your favorite beer style, a good place to research on your own is the Brewers Association website or Beer Advocate. For all styles, there are plenty of recipes to look at with a simple Google search, and once you've really gotten started with home brewing, you will be able to manipulate recipes to produce the style of beer you desire.

It is also worth noting that there are a few standards used for officially determining which style a beer is. The Brewers Association provides a full guide on many different styles, with very specific measurements for original gravity, final gravity, bitterness, color, and ABV, but we have here simply generated the most basic guidelines for some popular styles. These are by no means to be taken as law, as even between beer specialists, these guidelines are widely debated.

Ales

Ale is by far the oldest type of beer, and its main characteristic is that it uses what is known as a top-fermenting yeast. This simply means that the yeast settles at the top of the brew to work converting the sugars in the wort into ethanol and carbon dioxide. Top-fermenting yeast is often simply referred to as ale yeast. Typically, ales are stored at room temperature or warmer temperatures for a short period of time during the fermentation process. For a home brewer, an ale is much easier to brew. Ales are then further classified based on color, bitterness, ABV, and even the type of grain used. Ales tend to have more flowery and fruity flavors due to ale yeasts producing esters.

American Blonde Ale

Also called a golden ale, blonde ales are very light in color, ranging from straw to a very light amber. Blonde ale has between 15 and 25 IBU, and between 4.0% and 7.0% ABV. The hops flavor of a blonde ale is very low, and instead the malt flavor is more prominent. Blonde ales do not utilize many bittering hops, and generally use all pale ale malt, though sometimes different malts can be added for color. Hops are usually American. During the hour-long boil, steps should be taken to reduce caramelization of the malt. Yeast should be chosen to give blonde ales a clean finish.

American Brown Ale

American brown ales are, obviously, closer to brown in color, ranging from more coppery tones to very earthy browns. They have between 25 and 45 IBU, and between 4.0% to 6.3% ABV. They tend to have roasted malt, caramel, and chocolate flavors. Some American brown ales boast nutty flavors as well.

American India Pale Ale

American-style India pale ales have an IBU between 50-70, and they tend to be pale gold to amber or copper. Because their color has a fairly wide range, the malt extract used can vary. They generally fall between 5.5% and 7.5% ABV. American IPAs generally use American-grown hops, and hops are usually added at the beginning of the hour-long boil, and then more later to further develop flavor and aroma. Boiling hops unfortunately will break down the essential oils of the hops that provide a lot of aroma, which is why more can be added later in the boil or even in second fermentation. Bittering hops are hops added during the boil, while dry hops are added during second fermentation. The yeast should not really dominate the flavor profile.

American Pale Ale

American pale ales, or APAs, generally have a good balance of hops and malt, and are gold to copper in color. They tend to have an ABV of 4.0% to 5.4%, and are typically brewed with ingredients local to the region. The American version is usually hoppier than the British version and has a cleaner finish. IBU is usually between 30 and 50.

American Porter

The American porter is all black, and tends to be very bitter. It is between 35-50 IBU with a high hops bitterness. It has medium maltiness, low hops flavor, and tends to have between 7.0% and 12.0% ABV. Generally, it is brewed including chocolate or caramel malts to give it its dark color and characteristic flavors. It may also include black malt. You should use a yeast that provides a cleaner finish.

American Red Ale

American red ales are basically that – reddish-amber in color, with a balanced malt and hops profile. They are between 25-45 IBU, and usually American-grown hops are used. ABV is between 4.0% to 6.5%. They can have caramel and roasted malt notes, and occasionally light fruitiness.

American Stout

American stouts are black in color with a large head. Stouts have between 35-60 IBU, and between 5.5% and 9.0% ABV, and because of the addition of coffee or nuts, can also have these flavors present in the beer. Brewing tends to use more bittering hops, providing the higher IBU. However, the hops flavor is also high.

Belgian Pale Ale

Belgian-style pale ales are similar to their American and British counterparts. They are very similar to German pilseners. Traditionally, they are less bitter and are either gold or copper in color. They can fall between 20-50 IBU and 4% to 6.5% ABV.

Belgian Tripel

As the name would suggest, the Belgian Tripel uses triple the malt traditionally. They are extremely high ABV (typically between 7% and 12%), and are usually bottle conditioned. Their color is usually quite pale to light amber. The head of a Belgian Tripel is similar in consistency to mousse and is quite strong. IBU for a Tripel is between 20-45.

British India Pale Ale

A British-style India pale ale differs from its American cousin in its color and alcohol content, and also has far less of a hops flavor than American IPAs. Their IBU is between 35 and 63, and they have between 4.0% and 7.1% ABV. This style of IPA was developed by English sailors traveling between England and India. In brewing their beer, they simply added more hops to preserve it for the long journey, producing the IPA. Similarly to American IPAs, hops are added during the hour-long boil and potentially during second fermentation in order to produce the desired IBU content. British IPAs are paler in color than American IPAs.

Lagers

Unlike ales, lagers are fermented with bottom-fermenting yeast at a colder temperature. Instead of sitting at the top of the brew and consuming sugars, the yeast settles to the bottom of the brew to do so. Because of the colder temperature that they are fermented in (less than 50 degrees Fahrenheit), lagers take longer to ferment than ales. Lagers were developed much later as people became more able to control the climate in which their beers were fermented.

American Lager

American lager is typically straw or gold in color, with very little hops flavor. In fact, IBU for an American lager generally falls between 5-15. They traditionally have less alcohol content, with it capping out at around 5.5% ABV. They are clean, crisp, and very effervescent.

Bock

Bock is a German-style lager that is dark brown. They are traditionally made with all malt, with 20-30 IBU and between 5.5% to 8% ABV. They will have malty or roast aromas, but not caramel aromas. They are traditionally sweet and malty, with medium hops bitterness but low hops flavor.

German Dunkel

The German dunkel style tends to use German hops (noble-type hops, specifically) with Munich dark malt. The color of the dunkel is light brown to brown, and similar to porters, they can have chocolate or roasted malt aromas. IBU of the dunkel is between 16-25, while ABV is between 4.8-6%. They are well balanced beers.

German Pilsener

German-style pilseners are generally very pale in color with a dense, white head. There is a moderate hop flavor and aroma that should be immediately noticeable. Hops are usually added late in boiling rather than dry hopping. German pilseners have between 25-40 IBU with 4.0% to 5.5% ABV.

There are many, many more styles than those listed above, but these are common ones that are easily fit to standard brewing methods. There are also plenty of hybrids of beer, and there are also a number of sours out there that we have not mentioned.

Craft brewing and home brewing is a world that welcomes innovation and creativity in the process. The best beers out there are creations formed of true passion for brewing, and there are always new techniques and methods to explore. Many books much larger than this have been written about the art of home brewing, and hopefully, we have provided you a stable foundation to work from so that you can get started brewing your own craft beer from home.

The most important part of home brewing is to have fun and learn from mistakes. You could very well produce a sour batch of beer on your first try, and that's okay. Even the best brewers today can tell you a story of a batch that went bad. As long as you keep trying and have a passion for your craft, you will do just fine.

CONCLUSION

Thank for making it through to the end of *Home Brewing: A DIY Guide To Creating Your Own Craft Beer From Scratch*; we hope it was informative and able to provide you with all of the tools you need to achieve your beer-brewing goals, whatever they may be.

The next step is to go get your equipment and get started! The world of home brewing is chock full of creativity and innovation, and whether you are just looking to get into a new hobby or start a small-scale business; we hope that we have given you some insight into this wonderful industry. So long as there are passionate beer lovers in the world, there will be a thriving craft and home brew scene. In the beer industry, your voice certainly matters!

Finally, if you found this book useful in anyway, a review on Amazon is always appreciated!